A PLANNER AND A GUIDE

LIFE AND DEATH MATTERS

National Library of Australia Cataloguing-in-Publication entry

Author: Smith, Ammanda.

Title: Life and death matters / Ammanda Smith.

ISBN: 9780992577803 (paperback)

Subjects: Death--Handbooks, manuals, etc
Funeral rites and ceremonies.
Living wills--Handbooks, manuals, etc.
Advance directives (Medical care)--Handbooks, manuals, etc.

Dewey Number: 306.9

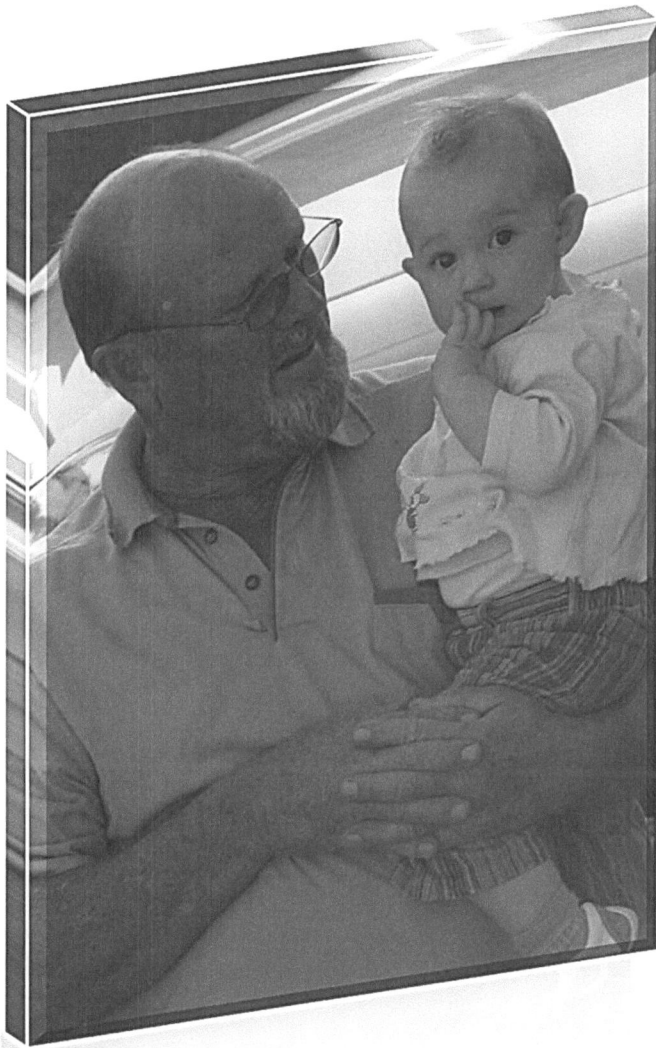

This book is dedicated to
My Dad
19th February 1950
3rd April 2014
I miss you every day

" Thinking of you is easy
I do it everyday.
Missing you is the heartache
that never goes away."

This subject is so taboo and nobody likes to
discuss it and face reality.
But the reality is - it happens to us all!

My Dad was taken so suddenly and
I would give anything just
to hear his voice, hold his hand,
and see his face again.

I thought Pa & I had another
10 or 20 years to discuss such
life-changing moments as these.

I urge you and your families to face it
before it becomes a reality.
If I can do one thing to make
it easier for someone else and to
honour Pa's memory:
this is it.

For those who know us, you will be aware of the recent loss and sudden death of my beloved Dad, Pa. During this time I discovered many things and I am still putting together a very big jigsaw puzzle. I have put this planner together to hopefully prevent others from having to go through what my family has.

I offer a simple and easy planner that every household should have. It will make things a little easier if you or those close to you are ever in this situation. It involves this book and your time to fill in the parts you think are relevant. No legal procedures, solicitors or funeral homes. You do not have to rely on memories or previous discussions.

We all have to face death eventually and it's those who are left behind that have to make plans and funeral arrangements. Many of you would have discussed this with your loved ones but at a time of loss and grief these details may not be remembered until later, after the shock has worn off.

Completing this simple planner can also prevent conflict and make your wishes clear.

Everyone's situation is different. Many people relocate, marry, divorce, have families, extend and blend their families. Life and Death Matters can be changed and updated whenever circumstances change or your wishes change.

It should be kept where it can be easily located should the worst case scenario happen. In certain circumstances it is not appropriate to go looking through a person's private documents or filing systems. If this guide is kept in a safe but accessible location then when it is required it can be easily found.
My suggestion would be in your medicine cabinet. Another option is to let someone know your special place or have them hold an additional copy.

I have included an "In Case of Emergency Card" that should be filled out and kept with your license, in your wallet or purse. It holds details of your next of kin and will notify your loved ones that this book has been filled in and where it can be found.

This book is not a funeral plan, will or estate plan. It is simply a guide to advise of your wishes. It may not be legally binding but if those close to you really love and respect you they will follow your wishes.

TABLE OF CONTENTS

Introduction v

Details 2

Next of Kin / Emergency Contact 4

Doctor / Medical Practitioner 5

My Wishes 6

Specific Instructions 6

At My Funeral I Would Like 8

The Service 10

Farewell / Wake 14

Expenses 14

Plan details 14

My Personal Instructions 16

Personal Information 18

Professional Contacts 22

Instructions for My Belongings 24

Who to Contact 28

Where to Find Things 30

Special Items I Wish to Pass 31

Relevant Genetic Medical History 33

Messages to Loved Ones 35

Statement 38

UPDATES

DETAILS	
Name	
Address	
Phone	
Email	
DOB	
Place of birth	

UPDATES

NEXT OF KIN / EMERGENCY CONTACT

Name	
Address	
Phone	
Email	
Relationship	
Second contact	

DOCTOR / MEDICAL SPECIALIST

Medical Practice **Doctors Name** **Address** **Phone**	
Specialist Practice **Doctors Name** **Address** **Phone**	
Other	

MY WISHES

I wish to be buried	Yes / No
Location	
I wish to be cremated	Yes / No
My ashes to be	

SPECIFIC INSTRUCTIONS

"Enjoy the little things in life,
for someday you will realise
they were big things."

AT MY FUNERAL I WOULD LIKE.......

Casket / coffin details	
Viewing	
Flowers	
Special items	
Music	
Donations to charities	

UPDATES

THE SERVICE

Service to be held at	
Religious or other service details	
Eulogy by	
Special word or verses	

UPDATES

THE SERVICE

Pallbearers	
Readings, prayers or poems	
Memorial / headstone	

UPDATES

FAREWELL / WAKE

Wake to be held at	
Specific instructions	

EXPENSES

Funeral expenses to be taken care of by	
Wake expenses to be taken care of by	

EXISTING FUNERAL PLAN

Funeral plan details & documents located	

This planner also contains a lot of relevant and very important information that people will need to know if you are not here to tell them.

MY PERSONAL INSTRUCTIONS

Organ donation **Australian Organ Donor Register** National register for people to record their decision about becoming an organ and tissue donor for transplantation after death.	Yes / No	Previous registration complete Yes / No
DNR request (Do not resuscitate)	Yes / No	Previous registration complete Yes / No
Advanced heath directive This document states your wishes or directions regarding your future health care for various medical conditions. It comes into effect only if you are unable to make your own decisions.	Yes / No	Previous registration complete Yes / No

For security reasons no account numbers or sensitive information is necessary in this section.

The institutions name and location of documents will help.

PERSONAL INFORMATION

My Will is located	
Last dated	
Executor / s	
Power of Attorney	
Enduring Power of Attorney	
Beneficiaries	
Estate Plan details and location	

UPPDATES

PERSONAL INFORMATION

Banking institution/s	
Credit card provider	
Home loan / mortgage	
Car loan and insurance	
Safety deposit box	
Life cover insurance provider	
Income protection provider	
House and contents insurance	

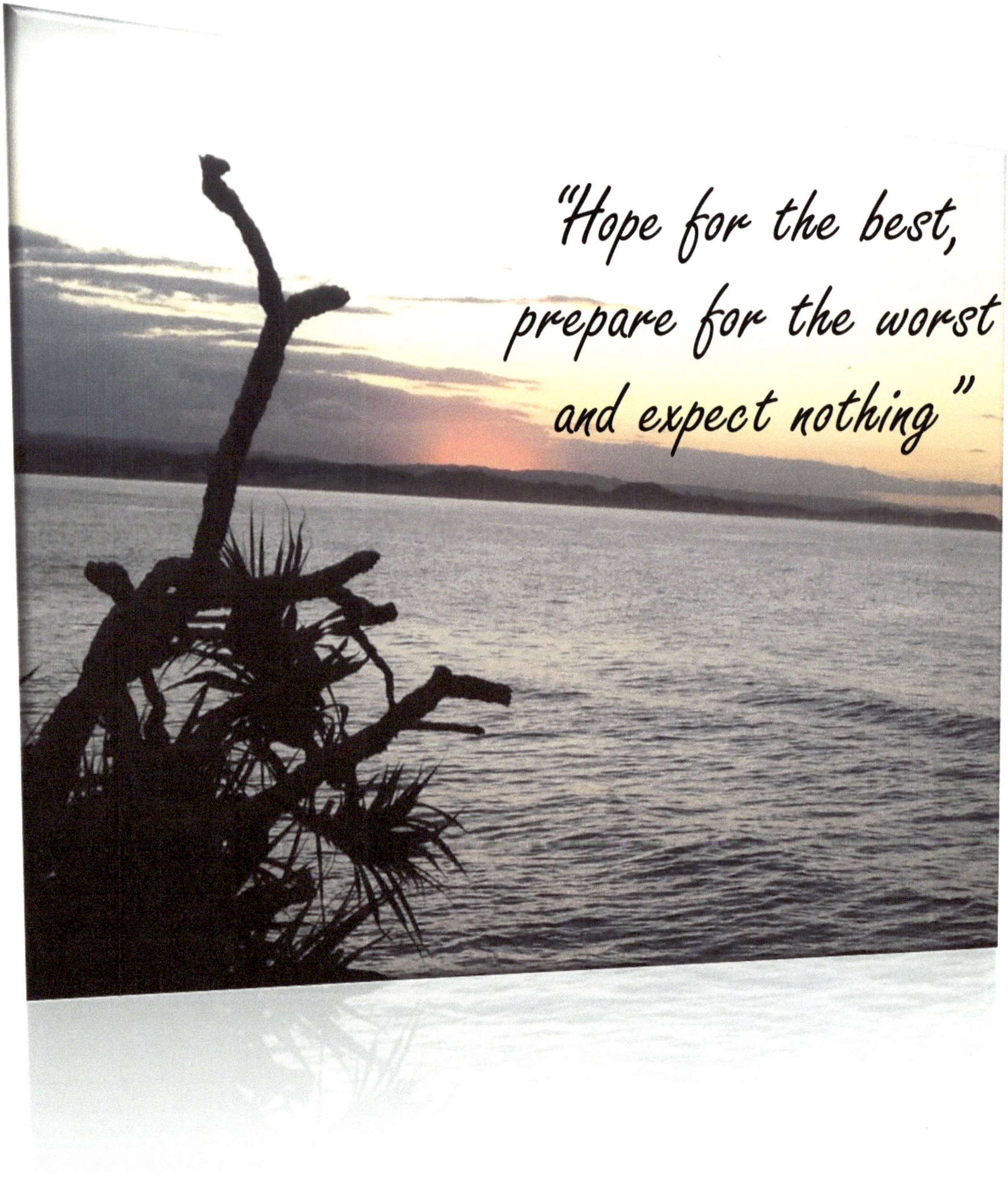
"Hope for the best,
prepare for the worst
and expect nothing"

PROFESSIONAL CONTACTS

Solicitor	
Lawyer	
Accountant	
Financial Planner	
Bank Manager	

UPDATES

INSTRUCTIONS FOR MY BELONGINGS

My children should be cared for by	
My pets should be cared for by	
My car/s should be cared for by	
My residence should be cared for by	
My agent for my rental property is	

UPDATES

INSTRUCTIONS

Business	
Investments	
Stocks / Shares	

UPDATES

WHO TO CONTACT	
Family	
Friends	
Workplace / employer	
Business associates	
Distant relatives	

This planner is not intended to be a substitute for a Will.
Some of this information should be included and documented
in a Will.
Many people do not have a current Will.
It is advisable that one is complete and the details of where
it is stored added to the relevant pages.

WHERE TO FIND THINGS	
Keys (including spare set)	
Computer details passwords	
Family heirlooms	
Photo albums or Storage device	

SPECIAL ITEMS I WISH TO PASS ON

SPECIAL ITEMS I WISH TO PASS ON

RELEVANT GENETIC MEDICAL HISTORY

RELEVANT GENETIC MEDICAL HISTORY

MESSAGES TO LOVED ONES

I _____

am of sound mind, and I have read and understood the importance of this book. Please respect my beliefs and values in life as we have previously discussed and documented.

I _____

hereby declare that the information completed in this book is a true record of my wishes on this date.

_____   _____
Signed   Date

_____   _____
Witness   Date

_____   _____
Witness Name   Relationship

www.ingramcontent.com/pod-product-compliance
Lightning Source LLC
Chambersburg PA
CBHW061050090426
42740CB00002B/98